This book belongs to:

*To my beloved four leaf clover, you know who you are,
and the universe, for your boundless inspiration.*

Text and Illustrations copyright © 2019 Venus Martinez Sharp

Published by Venus Martinez Sharp

All rights reserved.
No part of this publication may be reproduced, distributed, or transmitted in any form or by any means, including photocopying, recording, or other electronic or mechanical methods, without the prior written permission of the publisher, except in the case of brief quotations embodied in reviews and certain other noncommercial uses permitted by copyright law.

The moral right of the author and illustrator has been asserted.

Design and Illustrations by VM Ngo

ISBN 978-1-950638-00-0

Sami and the Orange Balloon

Adventures Over Campbell

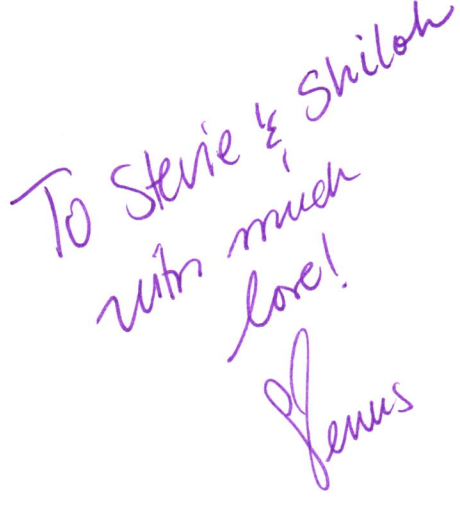

Venus Martinez Sharp

Sami woke up smiling with his orange crayon clenched in his fist.

After breakfast, he stepped outside, licked his fingertip, and held it up like a weather vane. The cool air hit his finger from the north, so the wind was heading south. As luck had it, his school was south from home.

Sami gathered his magic wand, goalie gloves, legos, cars, and orange crayon into his basket. He dragged it down the hall and thumped down the front door step.

Now, I just need a big balloon!

He stood on his toes as he used his crayon to draw a balloon, strings and hot orange flames. Then he climbed inside and lifted off the ground.

It was fun to see his house from the top, and the rows of rooftops. He could even see the clusters of buildings with funny names like Ebay and Netflix.

Not too far into the sky, he heard a sizzle and a roar. A hungry dragon was headed straight for him. He didn't have time to fight a dragon, he had to get to school!

Luckily, Sami knew just what to do. He pointed his wand and shouted his fire extinguishing incantation. The fire was put out and the dragon blew away.

Sami rose higher and higher until he came close to the moon. He wondered why it hadn't rolled away.

Down below, he heard a pair of blue jays arguing in the trees. Sami knew how to help.

Looking down at his gift, he noticed that it looked like a dandelion's airy seed head and he blew it instinctively. The stars dispersed back into the sky.

Not too far away, Sami spotted his brother Omar, so light on his feet, dribbling balls on the clouds.

He also saw Omar's skateboard and helmet and knew he must have rode an up-current for some soccer drills before school. Putting on his goalie gloves, Sami caught a few shots and continued riding the current toward school.

But a sudden crosswind blew the balloon west, away from school! He needed to stay on course, so he dug up some legos and built two wings and a control wheel.

Just then, his other brother Adam swooshed by on his own morning flight. Today he was flying his lego airplane.

Sami gave him a thumbs up and got one in return.

"I think he likes my wings," he decided.

As he saw his brother off, Sami caught sight of the town's tall water tower. He'd been curious about it for some time. He turned the balloon around, deciding firmly he'd take just a quick look because he couldn't be late for school.

When he reached the tower, he pulled himself close. He noticed the smooth steel tank, the ladder, and the tubing, but suddenly, his left wing hit the tank.

He gasped as he watched his lego pieces crumble down. "No!" he cried, "It's broken! How will I get to school now?"

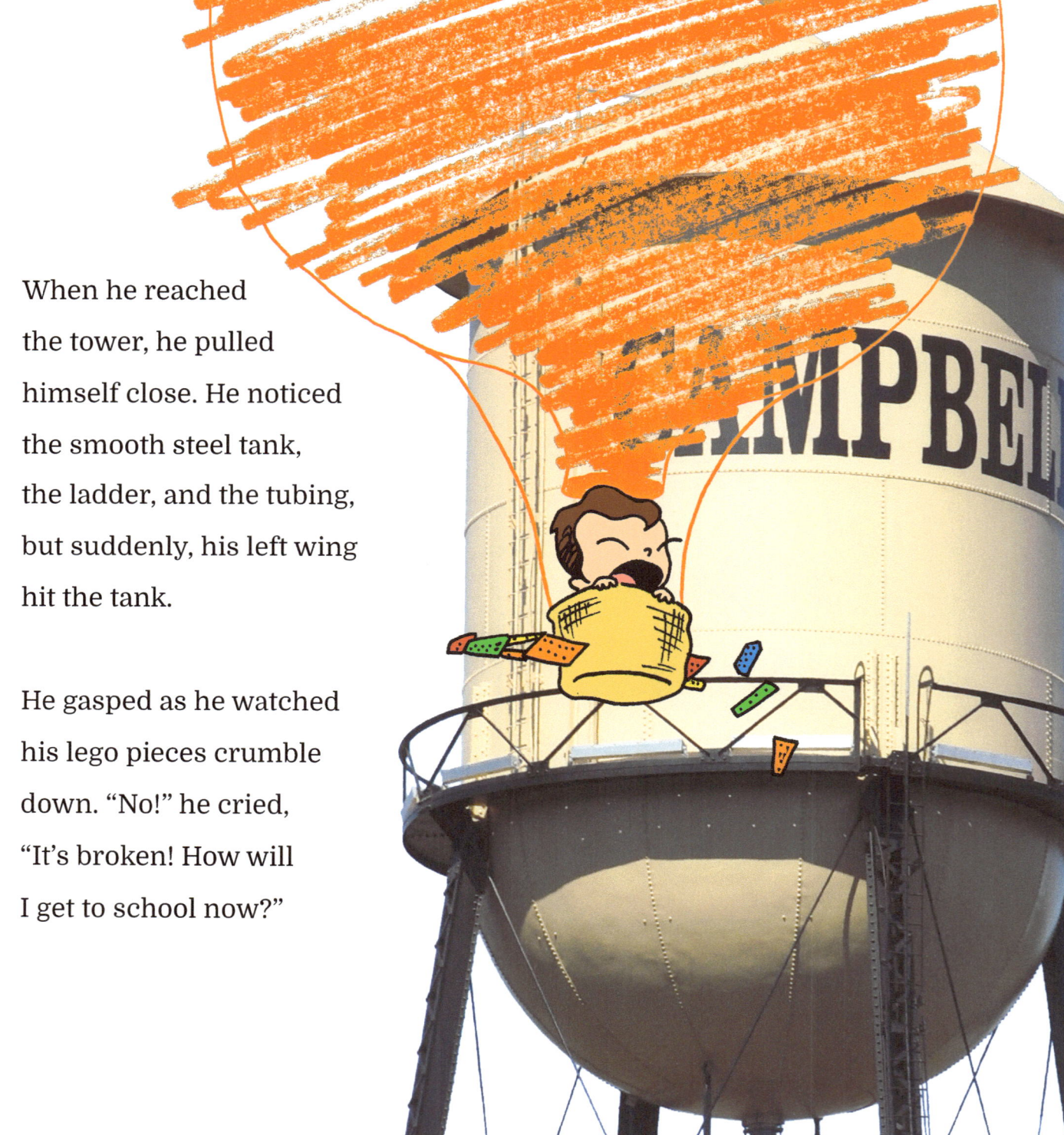

He searched the clouds for his brothers, but neither of them were within sight. Just then he remembered his cars. He opened the vent to his balloon, let out some of the hot air and began to descend.

On his descent, the balloon brushed a tree and caught some cherry blossoms in his basket.

As he continued down, he passed a traffic light and took the chance to color the dull yellow light a bright orange, something he had always wanted to do.

Upon landing, Sami collected his legos and removed the other wing. He turned the control wheel into a steering wheel and attached the cars to the underside of the basket. Then he set off driving down the street, making sure to stop for crossing squirrels.

He was making good time so he paused to greet an energetic dog on his morning walk. Sami was happy to find one last soccer ball in his basket. He tossed it to the surprised Maltipoo, sending him on a curious chase.

From the corner of his eye, he noticed something colorful floating above him.

What is that?

It was a kite with its string tied around a scroll and it seemed to be racing him to school.

Just then, he turned the corner, and saw his teachers greeting students in car-line. He was so glad to be on time. Now all he needed was a special song for his teachers. So he began to hum the tune of This Old Man and then he sang.

He searched the sky one last time and found the kite stuck in a tall evergreen. He smiled to himself knowing his next adventure awaited him.

VENUS MARTINEZ SHARP

simply lights up around children, stories, and the arts. So what better way to combine these passions than by creating and sharing children's books! She's a special education and Montessori trained teacher and lives with her husband and three boys in Campbell, California.

For more information and to download
a free coloring page visit:
venusmartinezsharp.com

CPSIA information can be obtained
at www.ICGtesting.com
Printed in the USA
LVHW070023281019
635510LV00005B/29/P